contents

British & North American Readers
Please note that Australian cup and spoon
measurements are metric. A quick conversion
guide appears on page 63.

about lettuce

Not so long ago, when a recipe asked for lettuce, there was only one type available: iceberg lettuce. Now you can buy lettuce with soft leaves, bitter leaves, red leaves and curly leaves, all of which makes our salads much more interesting.

iceberg lettuce
Firm, large, round head with crisp, pale-green leaves having a clean, grassy taste.

butter lettuce
Large and mild-tasting, its soft leaves are sweet and tender.

mignonette lettuce
Deep red or bright green tinged with red; firm, crisp leaves with a slightly bitter taste.

coral lettuce
Tightly furled, crunchy leaves with a mild but distinct taste. Red and green varieties.

oak leaf lettuce
Loosely packed, large-hearted lettuce with soft, gently frilled leaves with a mild flavour. Red and green varieties.

cos lettuce
Also called romaine, this crisp, elongated lettuce is the classic Caesar Salad green.

curly endive
A cousin of chicory, with a loose head of fine, spidery, slightly bitter, pale leaves.

mizuna
Feathery green leaves, edible pale stems; distinctive sharp flavour, often used in mesclun mixes.

radicchio
Red and bitter-tasting, add a few leaves to a mixed lettuce salad.

mesclun
Often sold as mixed salad leaves and consisting of an assortment of various edible greens.

lamb's lettuce
Also known as corn salad or mâche, it has clusters of tiny, tender, nutty-tasting leaves.

rocket
Also known as arugula; has nutty-tasting, soft leaves. Serve with other leaves or alone.

salad flowers
Several flowers have edible petals: roses, nasturtium, marigolds and violets. But be restrained, a few petals of one or two flowers is enough.

MIGNONETTE LETTUCE

CURLY ENDIVE

BUTTER LETTUCE

MIZUNA

LAMB'S LETTUCE

ICEBERG LETTUCE

CORAL LETTUCE

ROCKET

RADICCHIO

OAK LEAF LETTUCE

COS LETTUCE

MESCLUN

sweet chilli
prawn salad

Heat oil in large saucepan; deep-fry noodles, in batches, until puffed. Drain noodles on absorbent paper.

Shell and devein prawns, leaving tails intact. Heat sesame oil in wok or large frying pan; stir-fry garlic, onion, sprouts, capsicum, snow peas and prawns until prawns are tender and change colour.

Just before serving, gently toss prawn mixture and noodles in large bowl with Sweet Chilli Sauce.

Sweet Chilli Sauce Blend or process ingredients until well combined; transfer to small saucepan. Bring to a boil; simmer, uncovered, until sauce thickens slightly, stirring occasionally.

vegetable oil, for deep-frying

80g bean thread noodles

16 (400g) medium uncooked prawns

2 tablespoons sesame oil

2 cloves garlic, crushed

3 green onions, chopped

1 cup (80g) bean sprouts

1 small (150g) red capsicum, seeded, sliced

30g snow peas, sliced finely

sweet chilli sauce

6 small fresh red chillies, seeded, chopped

1 tablespoon sultanas

1 clove garlic, crushed

1 teaspoon grated fresh ginger

1 tablespoon white vinegar

1/4 cup (55g) caster sugar

1/2 teaspoon salt

1/4 cup (60ml) water

On the table in 50 minutes

tandoori

chicken salad

4 (680g) chicken
breast fillets

¹/₄ cup (65g)
tandoori paste

¹/₄ cup (60ml) yogurt

1 large (350g)
red capsicum

120g rocket, trimmed

250g cherry
tomatoes, halved

1 cup (100g)
walnuts, toasted

dressing

¹/₄ cup (60ml) olive oil

¹/₄ cup (60ml)
lime juice

2 tablespoons
mango chutney

Combine chicken, paste and yogurt in bowl. Cover;
refrigerate 10 minutes.
Quarter capsicum, remove seeds and membranes. Roast under
grill or in very hot oven, skin-side up, until skin blisters and
blackens. Cover capsicum pieces with plastic or paper for 5 minutes; peel
away skin. Cut capsicum into 1cm strips.
Drain chicken; discard marinade. Griddle-fry (or grill or barbecue)
chicken, in batches, until browned both sides and cooked through;
cool 5 minutes. Cut chicken into thin slices. Combine chicken,
capsicum and remaining ingredients in bowl; drizzle with Dressing.
Dressing Combine ingredients in screw-topped jar; shake well.
On the table in 30 minutes

cabanossi pasta salad

300g penne

2 sticks cabanossi, sliced

1 medium (200g) red capsicum, sliced

2 medium (240g) zucchini, sliced

4 green onions, sliced

1 tablespoon chopped fresh basil leaves

2 tablespoons finely grated parmesan cheese

1/2 cup (125ml) bottled Italian salad dressing

Cook pasta in large saucepan of boiling water, uncovered, until just tender; drain. **Combine** pasta with remaining ingredients in large bowl; toss together gently.

On the table in 25 minutes

spiced calamari salad

3 medium (600g)
calamari hoods

2 teaspoons grated
fresh ginger

2 cloves garlic,
crushed

$^1/_2$ teaspoon
cayenne pepper

1 tablespoon
chopped fresh
coriander leaves

$^1/_2$ teaspoon
five-spice powder

$^1/_4$ cup (60ml)
sweet chilli sauce

2 tablespoons olive oil

100g mesclun

dressing

$^1/_3$ cup (80ml) olive oil

2 tablespoons red
wine vinegar

2 teaspoons sugar

2 teaspoons lime juice

Cut calamari hoods open, cut shallow diagonal
slashes in criss-cross pattern on inside surface;
cut into 2cm x 6cm pieces. Combine calamari
with ginger, garlic, pepper, coriander, five-spice
powder and sauce in bowl. Cover; refrigerate
10 minutes.

Heat oil in wok; stir-fry calamari mixture, in
batches, about 1 minute or until tender. Serve
warm with mesclun; drizzle with Dressing.

Dressing Combine ingredients in screw-topped
jar; shake well.

On the table in 30 minutes

8 beef and noodle salad
with chilli lemon grass dressi

*500g beef eye-fillet
steaks*

300g hokkien noodles

*2 teaspoons
vegetable oil*

*500g baby bok choy,
chopped*

*500g choy sum,
chopped*

*1 bunch (500g)
Chinese broccoli,
chopped*

*1 small (400g)
Chinese cabbage,
shredded*

*1 cup (80g)
bean sprouts*

chilli lemon grass
dressing

*2 tablespoons
chopped lemon grass*

*2 small fresh red
chillies, seeded, sliced*

*2 tablespoons
soy sauce*

*2 tablespoons
lime juice*

*1 tablespoon grated
fresh ginger*

1 teaspoon sugar

Combine beef with one-third of the Chilli Lemon Grass Dressing in bowl. Cover; refrigerate 10 minutes.
Griddle-fry (or grill or barbecue) undrained beef, in batches, until browned all over and cooked as desired; cover, stand 5 minutes. Slice beef as desired.
Pour boiling water over noodles, stand 5 minutes; drain.
Heat oil in wok or large frying pan; quickly stir-fry bok choy, choy sum and broccoli until vegetables are just wilted.
Combine beef with noodles, vegetables, cabbage, sprouts and remaining Chilli Lemon Grass Dressing in bowl; toss together gently.
Chilli Lemon Grass Dressing
Combine ingredients in screw-topped jar; shake well.

On the table in 40 minutes

greek
potato salad

25 (1kg) tiny new potatoes, halved

1 medium (200g) red capsicum

1 medium (200g) yellow capsicum

2 small (260g) tomatoes, peeled

1 medium (170g) red onion, sliced

2/3 cup (100g) black olives, seeded

200g firm fetta cheese, chopped

dressing

1/3 cup (80ml) olive oil

1 tablespoon lemon juice

1 clove garlic, crushed

1 tablespoon chopped fresh dill

2 teaspoons chopped fresh thyme

Boil, steam or microwave potatoes until tender; drain and cool.

Quarter capsicums, remove seeds and membranes. Roast under grill or in very hot oven, skin-side up, until skin blisters and blackens. Cover capsicum pieces with plastic or paper for 5 minutes; peel away skin. Slice capsicum thickly.

Cut each tomato into 8 wedges. Combine ingredients with Dressing in bowl; mix gently.

Dressing Combine ingredients in screw-topped jar; shake well.

On the table in 30 minutes

sesame

chicken noodle salad

4 (680g) chicken
breast fillets, sliced

1 clove garlic, crushed

2 tablespoons sweet
chilli sauce

600g packet fresh
chow-mein style
noodles

1 (150g) baby
bok choy

1 medium (120g)
carrot

1 medium (200g)
red capsicum

1 tablespoon
peanut oil

250g asparagus,
trimmed, halved

2 teaspoons sesame
seeds, toasted

dressing

1/2 teaspoon
sesame oil

1/4 cup (60ml)
rice vinegar

2 tablespoons
soy sauce

1 tablespoon
lime juice

1 green onion, sliced

2 teaspoons sugar

Combine chicken, garlic and sauce in large
bowl. Cover; refrigerate 10 minutes.

Cook noodles in large saucepan of boiling
water, uncovered, until just tender; drain.

Cut leaves from bok choy. Cut bok choy stems,
carrot and capsicum into long thin strips.
Combine noodles, carrot and capsicum in
large bowl; mix well.

Heat oil in wok or large frying pan; stir-fry
chicken mixture, in batches, until browned
all over and tender. Add bok choy stems and
asparagus; stir-fry until asparagus is just tender.
Add bok choy leaves; stir-fry until just wilted.
Add chicken mixture to noodle mixture; mix well.
Drizzle with Dressing; sprinkle with seeds.

Dressing Combine ingredients in screw-topped
jar; shake well.

On the table in 40 minutes

12 chicken and
coriander salad

You will need 1 large cooked chicken for this recipe.

2¹/₂ cups (425g) chopped cooked chicken

500g spinach, trimmed

100g snow pea sprouts

1 medium (200g) red capsicum, chopped

4 green onions, chopped

250g cherry tomatoes, halved

1 (130g) Lebanese cucumber, sliced

¹/₄ cup chopped fresh coriander leaves

dressing

¹/₃ cup (80ml) vegetable oil

1 tablespoon soy sauce

2 tablespoons sweet chilli sauce

¹/₂ teaspoon sesame oil

¹/₄ cup (60ml) white vinegar

¹/₂ teaspoon sugar

Combine chicken with torn spinach leaves and remaining ingredients in large bowl. Just before serving, add warm Dressing; toss gently.
Dressing Combine ingredients in small saucepan; whisk over heat until warm. Do not boil.

On the table in 30 minutes

indonesian

salad

1/4 cup (60ml) peanut oil

375g packet firm tofu, drained, sliced

1/2 small (200g) Chinese cabbage, shredded finely

1 large (500g) kumara

150g snow peas

1 1/2 cups (120g) bean sprouts

4 hard-boiled eggs, quartered

1 (130g) Lebanese cucumber, sliced thinly

1/4 cup loosely packed fresh coriander leaves

peanut sauce

3/4 cup (110g) unsalted roasted peanuts

1 1/4 cups (310ml) coconut milk

2 green onions, chopped

1/4 cup (65g) smooth peanut butter

2 tablespoons fish sauce

1 teaspoon sambal oelek

2 teaspoons sugar

Heat 2 tablespoons of the oil in non-stick frying pan; cook tofu until browned both sides, drain on absorbent paper.
Heat remaining oil in same pan; cook cabbage, stirring, until just wilted, cool.
Slice kumara into long, thin strips. Boil, steam or microwave kumara and snow peas separately until just tender; drain. Rinse under cold water; drain well.
Just before serving, arrange kumara on serving plate; drizzle with a little of the Peanut Sauce. Repeat layering with remaining vegetables, eggs, tofu and Peanut Sauce. Serve topped with coriander leaves.
Peanut Sauce Process nuts until chopped roughly. Add remaining ingredients; process until combined.

On the table in 40 minutes

14 lamb and bean
parmesan salad

500g lamb eye of loin
200g green beans, chopped
200g butter beans, chopped
350g watercress, trimmed
1 medium (170g) red onion, sliced

parmesan dressing

^{1}/$_2$ cup (40g) finely grated parmesan cheese

^{1}/$_2$ cup chopped fresh flat-leaf parsley

^{1}/$_2$ cup (125ml) olive oil

^{1}/$_2$ cup (125ml) white wine vinegar

2 cloves garlic, crushed

Griddle-fry (or grill or barbecue) lamb, until browned all over and cooked as desired. Remove from pan, cover; stand 5 minutes. Slice lamb thinly.
Boil, steam or microwave both beans until just tender, rinse under cold water; drain. Combine lamb with beans, watercress and onion in large bowl; drizzle with Parmesan Dressing.
Parmesan Dressing Blend or process ingredients until smooth and creamy.

On the table in 35 minutes

16 gingered
pork salad

500g lean pork strips

3 teaspoons grated
fresh ginger

3 teaspoons
sesame oil

1 tablespoon
soy sauce

1 tablespoon
cider vinegar

3 (450g) baby
bok choy

250g snow peas

1 tablespoon finely
grated lime rind

$1/4$ cup (60ml)
lime juice

2 tablespoons
chopped fresh
coriander leaves

$2^1/2$ cups (200g)
bean sprouts

Combine pork with ginger, half of the oil, half
of the sauce and half of the vinegar in bowl,
cover; refrigerate 10 minutes.
Discard stems from bok choy. Cover bok choy
and peas with boiling water; stand 2 minutes.
Drain, rinse under cold water; drain.
Cook undrained pork, in batches, in heated non-
stick frying pan, stirring, until tender.
Combine remaining oil, sauce and vinegar with
rind, juice and coriander in screw-topped jar;
shake well. Toss ingredients together in bowl.
Top with chives and chopped chilli, if desired.

On the table in 45 minutes

chicken and
COUSCOUS salad

2/3 cup (160ml) water

20g butter

2/3 cup (130g) couscous

2 teaspoons finely grated lemon rind

1/3 cup (90g) pesto with sun-dried tomatoes

2 tablespoons lemon juice

1 tablespoon vegetable oil

10 (750g) chicken tenderloins

240g rocket, trimmed

Bring water to a boil in medium saucepan; remove from heat. Stir in butter, couscous and rind; cover, stand 2 minutes or until water is absorbed. Fluff couscous with fork. Whisk pesto with juice in small bowl until combined. **Heat** oil in large frying pan; cook chicken, in batches, until browned and cooked through. **Combine** couscous with pesto mixture, chicken and rocket in bowl; toss well.

On the table in 40 minutes

18 barbecued pork
and rice salad

You will need to cook 1 cup (200g) brown rice for this recipe.

100g snow peas, halved

3 cups cooked brown rice

425g can baby corn, drained, chopped

230g can water chestnuts, drained, halved

1 small (150g) red capsicum, chopped

4 green onions, chopped

150g Chinese barbecued pork, sliced

1 tablespoon sesame seeds, toasted

dressing

1/4 cup (60ml) peanut oil

2 teaspoons sesame oil

1 teaspoon soy sauce

1/4 cup (60ml) rice vinegar

1 clove garlic, crushed

1/2 teaspoon brown sugar

Boil, steam or microwave snow peas until just tender; drain. **Combine** snow peas, rice, corn, chestnuts, capsicum, onion and pork in bowl. Add **Dressing**; mix well. Sprinkle with seeds. Dressing Combine ingredients in screw-topped jar; shake well.

On the table in 40 minutes

thai-style

prawn, mango and tomato salad

20 (1kg) large
cooked prawns

3 large (1.8kg)
mangoes, chopped

1 large (300g) red
onion, sliced

1/3 cup firmly packed
fresh coriander leaves

500g cherry
tomatoes, halved

660g yellow teardrop
tomatoes, halved

2 tablespoons sesame
seeds, toasted

2 large (640g)
avocados, sliced

dressing

1 clove garlic, crushed

1 small fresh red chilli,
seeded, quartered

1 medium (190g)
tomato, peeled,
quartered

2 tablespoons
lime juice

1 teaspoon sugar

2 teaspoons
rice vinegar

2 teaspoons chopped
fresh coriander leaves

1/4 cup (60ml)
peanut oil

1 teaspoon grated
fresh ginger

Shell and devein
prawns, leaving tails
intact. Combine
prawns with remaining
ingredients in large
bowl; add Dressing,
toss gently. Serve on
watercress, if desired.
Dressing Blend or
process ingredients
until smooth.

On the table in 45 minutes

lamb antipasto
salad

2 medium (400g)
red capsicums

200g button
mushrooms

4 medium (300g) egg
tomatoes, halved

500g lamb eye of loin

1/2 cup (80g) black
olives, seeded

200g bottled
char-grilled
eggplant, drained

1 medium (200g)
radicchio lettuce

250g bocconcini
cheese, sliced

dressing

1/3 cup (80ml) olive oil

2 tablespoons
balsamic vinegar

1 tablespoon shredded
fresh basil leaves

1 clove garlic, crushed

Quarter capsicums, remove seeds and membranes. Roast under grill or in very hot oven, skin-side up, until skin blisters and blackens. Cover capsicum pieces with plastic or paper for 5 minutes; peel away skin. Halve capsicum pieces.

Griddle-fry (or grill or barbecue) mushrooms and tomatoes, in batches, brushing with a little of the Dressing, until browned on both sides and tender. Add lamb to same pan, brush with a little more of the Dressing; cook until browned both sides and cooked as desired. Cover, stand 5 minutes, slice.

Place capsicum, mushrooms, tomatoes, lamb, olives, eggplant, radicchio and bocconcini on platter; drizzle with remaining Dressing.

Dressing Combine ingredients in screw-topped jar; shake well.

On the table in 35 minutes

22 classic chef's
salad

350g chicken
breast fillets

3 medium (225g)
egg tomatoes

1 large cos lettuce

200g finely sliced
leg ham

100g finely sliced
Jarlsberg cheese

3 hard-boiled eggs,
quartered

vinaigrette

1/2 cup (125ml)
olive oil

1/4 cup (60ml) white
wine vinegar

2 teaspoons
seeded mustard

1 teaspoon sugar

1/4 teaspoon
cracked pepper

Cook chicken in heated oiled large frying
pan until browned both sides.
Place chicken in shallow baking dish;
bake, uncovered, in moderate oven about
15 minutes or until cooked through. Cool
5 minutes; cut into thin slices.
Cut each tomato into 8 wedges. Wash and
separate lettuce leaves; tear into small pieces.
Divide lettuce among serving bowls; layer
with chicken, tomato, ham, cheese and egg,
then drizzle with vinaigrette.
Vinaigrette Combine ingredients in
screw-topped jar; shake well.

On the table in 35 minutes

baby spinach, potato and egg salad

Combine potatoes and 2 tablespoons of the oil in large baking dish; bake, uncovered, in very hot oven 25 minutes.

Meanwhile, cover eggs with water in medium saucepan; bring to a boil. Simmer, uncovered, 10 minutes; drain. Rinse eggs under cold water; shell and cut into quarters.

Cook bacon in large heated dry frying pan until crisp; drain on absorbent paper

Gently toss bacon in large bowl with potatoes, eggs and spinach. Blend or process remaining ingredients, drizzle over salad.

18 (720g) tiny new potatoes, halved

$1/2$ cup (125ml) olive oil

6 eggs

4 bacon rashers, chopped

200g baby spinach leaves

2 tablespoons white wine vinegar

4 anchovy fillets in oil, drained

2 tablespoons coarsely grated parmesan cheese

On the table in 40 minutes

24 tomato, bocconcini and
lamb salad

2 (800g) lamb mini roasts

2 medium (380g) tomatoes, sliced

1/4 cup firmly packed fresh
basil leaves

250g bocconcini cheese, sliced

1/2 cup (125ml) light olive oil

2 tablespoons red wine vinegar

2 teaspoons Dijon mustard

1 teaspoon sugar

1 clove garlic, crushed

2 teaspoons olive paste

Place lamb in large oiled baking
dish; bake, uncovered, in moderate
oven about 25 minutes or until
cooked as desired. Cover lamb,
stand 5 minutes; slice thinly.
Layer lamb, tomato, basil and
bocconcini on platter; drizzle with
combined remaining ingredients.

On the table in 45 minutes

ham and
crisp potato salad

25 (1kg) tiny new potatoes, halved

2 teaspoons olive oil

1 tablespoon lemon pepper seasoning

180g green beans

400g lean leg ham, sliced thinly

100g mesclun

1 large (320g) avocado, chopped

1/2 cup (125ml) orange juice

2 tablespoons lemon juice

2 teaspoons Dijon mustard

1 teaspoon balsamic vinegar

1 clove garlic, crushed

1 teaspoon caster sugar

Combine potatoes, oil and seasoning in large non-stick baking dish; bake, uncovered, in very hot oven about 25 minutes or until browned and tender. Boil, steam or microwave beans until just tender, rinse under cold water; drain.

Combine potatoes, beans, ham, mesclun and avocado in bowl.

Combine remaining ingredients in screw-topped jar; shake well. Drizzle over salad just before serving.

On the table in 45 minutes

250g asparagus, trimmed, chopped

200g snow peas, halved

100g bean thread noodles

1 (130g) Lebanese cucumber

1 medium (120g) carrot

2 cups (160g) bean sprouts

1 medium (200g) red capsicum, sliced thinly

4 green onions, chopped

2 tablespoons chopped fresh mint leaves

2 tablespoons chopped fresh coriander leaves

3 (500g) beef rib-eye steaks

1/3 cup (50g) unsalted roasted peanuts

1/4 cup fresh coriander leaves, extra

dressing

1/3 cup (80ml) sweet chilli sauce

2 tablespoons lime juice

2 tablespoons peanut oil

2 teaspoons fish sauce

1 clove garlic, crushed

Place asparagus and snow peas in medium heatproof bowl, cover with boiling water, stand 2 minutes; drain. Rinse under cold water; drain well. Place noodles in medium heatproof bowl, cover with boiling water, stand 5 minutes; drain.
Cut cucumber in half lengthways, scoop out seeds; slice thinly. Cut carrot lengthways into long strips using a vegetable peeler.
Toss asparagus, snow peas, noodles, cucumber, carrot, sprouts, capsicum, onion, mint, coriander and Dressing in large bowl.
Meanwhile, griddle-fry (or grill or barbecue) beef, until browned both sides and cooked as desired. Cover, stand 10 minutes; slice thinly. Toss beef through salad; top with nuts and extra coriander.
Dressing Combine ingredients in screw-topped jar; shake well.

On the table in 45 minutes

28 tofu vegetable
salad

375g packet firm tofu, drained

*2/3 cup (160ml) bottled Italian
salad dressing*

2 medium (240g) zucchini

2 medium (240g) carrots

1 medium (200g) red capsicum

500g spinach, trimmed

250g cherry tomatoes

2 tablespoons chopped fresh chives

*1/2 cup (40g) flaked
parmesan cheese*

Cut tofu into 2cm cubes,
combine tofu with dressing
in bowl. Cover; refrigerate
10 minutes.
Cut zucchini, carrots and
capsicum into long thin strips.
Combine tofu mixture with
vegetables and remaining
ingredients in large bowl;
toss gently to mix.

On the table in 35 minutes

satay

beef salad

500g piece beef eye-fillet

2 medium (240g) carrots

3 cups (240g)
bean sprouts

100g snow pea
sprouts

1 medium
(170g) red
onion, sliced

1/4 cup loosely
packed fresh
coriander
leaves

1/3 cup (50g)
chopped unsalted
roasted peanuts

satay sauce

2 tablespoons
brown sugar

2 tablespoons chopped
fresh coriander leaves

1/4 cup (60ml) sweet
chilli sauce

1/2 cup (130g) smooth
peanut butter

2 cloves garlic, crushed

1/2 cup (125ml)
coconut milk

1/2 cup (125ml) water

Griddle-fry (or grill or barbecue) beef,
uncovered, about 20 minutes or until
browned all over and cooked as desired.
Cover beef; stand 10 minutes before
cutting into thin slices.

Cut carrots lengthways into long thin strips,
using a vegetable peeler. Combine carrot,
beef, sprouts and onion in bowl, drizzle
with Satay Sauce; sprinkle with coriander
leaves and peanuts.

Satay Sauce Combine ingredients in
small saucepan; simmer, stirring, until
sauce thickens, cool slightly.

On the table in 45 minutes

30 prawn salad with
citrus dressing

60 (1.5kg) medium uncooked prawns

1/2 loaf (400g) unsliced white bread

2 tablespoons olive oil

500g asparagus, trimmed, chopped

1 baby cos lettuce

2 medium (500g) avocados, chopped

citrus dressing

1 teaspoon grated orange rind

1/3 cup (80ml) orange juice

1 teaspoon grated lemon rind

1 tablespoon lemon juice

1/4 cup (60ml) mayonnaise

2 tablespoons olive oil

1 tablespoon balsamic vinegar

2 teaspoons sugar

1 clove garlic, chopped

Shell and devein prawns, leaving tails intact. Combine prawns with 1/4 cup (60ml) of the Citrus Dressing in bowl; cover, refrigerate 10 minutes.

Cut crusts from bread; cut bread into 2cm cubes. Combine cubes with oil in bowl; mix well. Place bread, in single layer, in shallow baking dish; bake, uncovered, in moderately hot oven about 15 minutes or until croutons are browned and crisp, stirring occasionally.

Boil, steam or microwave asparagus until just tender, rinse under cold water; drain.

Drain prawns; discard marinade. Griddle-fry (or grill or barbecue) prawns, in batches, until browned both sides and just cooked.

Combine prawns with croutons, asparagus, lettuce leaves, avocado and remaining Citrus Dressing in large bowl; mix gently.

Citrus Dressing Blend or process ingredients until smooth.

On the table in 50 minutes

chicken, cucumber

and sprout salad

*1¹/₄ cups (310ml)
chicken stock*

*¹/₄ cup (60ml)
lime juice*

*¹/₄ cup (60ml)
dry white wine*

*3 (500g) chicken
breast fillets*

*1 large (400g)
cucumber*

*200g fresh
egg noodles*

*1¹/₂ cups (120g)
bean sprouts*

*2 small fresh red
chillies, seeded, sliced*

*1 tablespoon chopped
fresh coriander leaves*

*1 tablespoon lime
juice, extra*

*¹/₄ cup (60ml) light
olive oil*

*1 tablespoon sweet
chilli sauce*

*1 tablespoon
rice vinegar*

*2 teaspoons
hoisin sauce*

1 teaspoon soy sauce

On the table in 45 minutes

Combine stock, juice, wine and chicken in
large saucepan. Bring to a boil; simmer, covered,
about 20 minutes or until chicken is just tender.
Remove chicken from stock; when cool enough
to handle, slice thinly. Discard stock.
Halve cucumber, remove seeds; slice cucumber
diagonally. Cook noodles in large saucepan
of boiling water, uncovered, until just tender;
drain. Rinse under cold water; drain.
Gently toss chicken, cucumber and noodles in
large bowl with sprouts, chillies, coriander, extra
juice and combined remaining ingredients.

dazzling dressings

Even a simple lettuce salad becomes a treat when tossed with a well-flavoured dressing. Here are four of the classics; you'll find more throughout the book.

italian dressing

1/2 cup (125ml) white vinegar

1 tablespoon lemon juice

1 teaspoon sugar

1/2 cup (125ml) light olive oil

1 clove garlic, crushed

1/2 small (40g) white onion, chopped finely

1/2 small (75g) red capsicum, chopped finely

1/4 cup chopped flat-leaf parsley

Combine ingredients in screw-topped jar; shake well.
Makes about
2/3 cup (160ml).

thousand island dressing

1 cup (250ml) mayonnaise

1/4 cup (60ml) tomato paste

1/4 cup (60ml) tomato sauce

2 teaspoons Worcestershire sauce

1/2 teaspoon Tabasco sauce

Combine ingredients in small bowl; whisk until smooth. Cover and refrigerate until required.
Makes about
1 1/2 cups (375ml).

honey dijon dressing

1/4 cup (60ml) honey

2 tablespoons Dijon mustard

1/2 cup (125ml) white wine vinegar

1 tablespoon lemon juice

1 cup (250ml) peanut oil

Combine honey, mustard, vinegar and juice in small bowl. Gradually whisk in oil; continue to whisk until dressing is slightly thickened and smooth.
Makes about
2/3 cup (160ml).

Dressings from left: Honey Dijon, French, Italian, Thousand Island.

french dressing

1/2 cup (125ml) olive oil

1 tablespoon white wine vinegar

2 teaspoons Dijon mustard

1/2 teaspoon sugar

Combine ingredients in screw-topped jar; shake well. Makes about 2/3 cup (160ml).

lamb salad
niçoise

2 large pieces pitta

1 tablespoon olive oil

500g lamb eye of loin

150g green beans

1 baby cos lettuce

150g curly endive

400g radishes,
sliced thinly

1 medium (170g)
red onion, sliced

4 hard-boiled eggs,
quartered

8 anchovy fillets
in oil, drained

buttermilk dressing

1/2 cup (125ml) light
olive oil

2 cloves garlic,
chopped coarsely

2 tablespoons white
wine vinegar

1 teaspoon sugar

2 tablespoons
chopped fresh
basil leaves

1/2 cup (125ml)
buttermilk

Place pitta on oven tray; toast, uncovered, in moderately hot oven about 10 minutes or until crisp. Cool pitta; break into pieces.
Heat oil in large frying pan; cook lamb, uncovered, until browned all over and cooked as desired. Stand lamb, covered, 5 minutes; slice thinly.
Boil, steam or microwave beans until just tender; drain. Rinse under cold water; drain.
Just before serving, gently toss pitta pieces, lamb and beans in large bowl with lettuce, endive, radish, onion, eggs, anchovy fillets and Buttermilk Dressing.
Buttermilk Dressing Blend or process ingredients until smooth.

On the table in 45 minutes

lime, tomato and
scallop salad

*250g dried
rice noodles*

500g white scallops

*1 tablespoon sweet
chilli sauce*

*1 tablespoon
lime juice*

*250g asparagus,
trimmed, chopped*

*330g yellow teardrop
tomatoes, halved*

*1/3 cup (25g) flaked
almonds, toasted*

lime dressing

*1/2 cup (125ml)
peanut oil*

*1 teaspoon
brown sugar*

*2 tablespoons
chopped fresh
coriander leaves*

*1 tablespoon chopped
fresh mint leaves*

*2 small fresh red
chillies, seeded,
quartered*

*1/4 cup (60ml)
lime juice*

On the table in 40 minutes

Place noodles in large heatproof bowl, cover with boiling water, stand only until just tender; drain. Rinse under cold water; drain.
Griddle-fry (or grill or barbecue) scallops, in batches, until changed in colour, occasionally brushing with combined chilli sauce and juice. Boil, steam or microwave asparagus until just tender; rinse under cold water, drain.
Gently toss noodles, scallops and asparagus in large bowl with tomato and Lime Dressing; sprinkle with nuts.
Lime Dressing Blend or process ingredients until smooth.

36 avocado and bacon
pasta salad

400g penne

2 teaspoons olive oil

6 bacon rashers, chopped

2 cloves garlic, crushed

2 large (700g) red capsicums

250g cherry tomatoes, halved

3 medium (750g) avocados, chopped

120g rocket, trimmed

dressing

2 tablespoons lemon juice

3/4 cup (180ml) light sour cream

3/4 cup firmly packed fresh basil leaves

Cook pasta in large saucepan of boiling water, uncovered, until just tender; drain. Rinse under cold water; drain.

Heat oil in frying pan; cook bacon and garlic, stirring, until bacon is crisp. Drain on absorbent paper.

Quarter capsicums, remove seeds and membranes. Roast under grill or in very hot oven, skin-side up, until skin blisters and blackens. Cover capsicum pieces with plastic or paper for 5 minutes; peel away skin. Cut capsicum into 2cm strips.

Just before serving, combine pasta with the bacon mixture, capsicum, tomato, avocado and rocket; drizzle with Dressing.

Dressing Blend or process ingredients until smooth and creamy.

On the table in 35 minutes

fetta, tomato and
chickpea salad

200g firm fetta cheese, chopped

2 medium (380g) tomatoes, seeded, sliced

2 x 300g cans chickpeas, rinsed, drained

125g baby spinach leaves

²/₃ cup (160ml) bottled Italian salad dressing

*¹/₄ cup firmly packed fresh basil
leaves, shredded*

Combine ingredients
in large bowl;
mix well.

On the table in 20 minutes

grilled haloumi,

tomato and eggplant salad

¹/₂ cup (125ml) olive oil
4 (240g) baby eggplants, sliced
4 medium (300g) egg tomatoes, halved lengthways
400g haloumi cheese, sliced thinly
250g rocket, trimmed, chopped coarsely
¹/₄ cup firmly packed fresh basil leaves
2 tablespoons red wine vinegar
1 tablespoon drained capers, chopped

Heat 1 tablespoon of the oil in large frying pan or griddle;
cook eggplant until browned both sides. Remove from pan.
Add tomato to same pan; cook, cut-side down, until browned
and softened slightly. Remove from pan.
Heat another tablespoon of the oil in same pan; cook haloumi
until browned lightly both sides.
Combine eggplant, tomato, haloumi, rocket and basil in large bowl
with remaining oil, vinegar and capers.

On the table in 40 minutes

caesar salad

40cm bread stick

60g butter, melted

1 tablespoon olive oil

2 cloves garlic, crushed

4 bacon rashers, chopped

2 (340g) chicken breast fillets

1 cos lettuce

1/2 cup (40g) flaked parmesan cheese

caesar dressing

1 egg

1 clove garlic, crushed

2 tablespoons lemon juice

1 teaspoon Dijon mustard

1/4 cup (20g) grated parmesan cheese

1/2 x 45g can anchovy fillets, drained

3/4 cup (180ml) olive oil

Cut bread into 4cm pieces. Combine bread, butter, oil and garlic in large bowl; mix well. Place bread on oven tray; bake, uncovered, in moderate oven about 10 minutes or until browned and crisp; cool.

Cook bacon in non-stick frying pan, stirring, until crisp; drain on absorbent paper. Cook chicken in same pan until browned both sides and cooked through; slice.

Combine lettuce leaves with bacon, chicken, croutons and cheese; drizzle with Caesar Dressing.

Caesar Dressing Blend or process egg, garlic, juice, mustard, cheese and anchovies until smooth. Gradually add oil, while motor is operating; blend or process until thick.

On the table in 40 minutes

lamb

and macadamia nut salad

500g lamb eye of loin

1/4 cup (60ml) dry
red wine

2 cloves garlic,
crushed

4 large (360g) egg
tomatoes, quartered

1 tablespoon olive oil

1/2 teaspoon sugar

1/2 teaspoon ground
black pepper

1/4 cup (60ml) red
wine vinegar

1 teaspoon
Dijon mustard

1 clove garlic, chopped
coarsely

1/4 cup (20g) coarsely
grated parmesan
cheese

1/4 cup (60ml)
macadamia oil

1 tablespoon chopped
fresh basil leaves

1/2 cup (75g)
macadamia nuts,
toasted, chopped

250g rocket, trimmed

On the table in 50 minutes

Combine lamb, wine and crushed garlic in
large bowl. Cover; refrigerate 10 minutes.
Place tomato on oven tray; drizzle with olive
oil, sprinkle with sugar and pepper. Bake,
uncovered, in very hot oven about 10 minutes
or until tomato is soft.
Drain lamb over medium bowl; reserve
marinade. Cook lamb, uncovered, in large
heated oiled frying pan until browned all over
and cooked as desired. Cover lamb, stand
5 minutes; slice thinly.
Add marinade to same pan; bring to a
boil. Simmer, uncovered, until reduced to
1 tablespoon; blend or process with vinegar,
mustard, chopped garlic, cheese, macadamia
oil and basil until smooth.
Gently toss lamb, tomato, nuts and rocket
in large bowl with dressing.

42 sesame beef salad

500g piece beef
eye-fillet

1 teaspoon grated
fresh ginger

1 clove garlic, crushed

1/4 cup (60ml)
soy sauce

1/4 cup (60ml)
sweet sherry

2 tablespoons
sesame oil

250g asparagus,
trimmed, chopped

150g snow peas

250g dried wheat
noodles

1 teaspoon
Dijon mustard

2 teaspoons honey

1 tablespoon white
wine vinegar

2 tablespoons olive oil

3 green onions, sliced

1 tablespoon sesame
seeds, toasted

Combine beef with ginger, garlic, sauce, sherry and sesame oil in large bowl. Cover; refrigerate 10 minutes. **Boil,** steam or microwave asparagus and snow peas, separately, until just tender; drain. Rinse, drain well.

Cook noodles in large saucepan of boiling water, uncovered, until just tender; drain. Rinse under cold water; drain again.

Drain beef over medium bowl; reserve marinade. Cook beef in large heated oiled frying pan until browned both sides and cooked as desired. Remove from pan; cover, stand 10 minutes, slice thinly. Add marinade to same pan. Simmer, uncovered, about 2 minutes or until mixture thickens.

Combine marinade with mustard, honey, vinegar and olive oil in large bowl. Just before serving, gently toss beef, asparagus, snow peas and noodles with marinade mixture, onion and sesame seeds.

On the table in 50 minutes

tuna salad with beans

1 medium (200g) red capsicum

9 (360g) tiny new potatoes, halved

300g green beans

2 medium (380g) tomatoes, chopped

1 small butter lettuce

425g can tuna, drained

2 hard-boiled eggs, quartered

1/4 cup (40g) black olives, seeded

herb dressing

1/2 cup (125ml) olive oil

1/4 cup (60ml) balsamic vinegar

1 tablespoon Dijon mustard

1/4 cup shredded fresh basil leaves

1 tablespoon chopped fresh thyme

Quarter capsicum, remove seeds and membranes. Roast under grill or in very hot oven, skin-side up, until skin blisters and blackens. Cover capsicum pieces with plastic or paper for 5 minutes; peel away skin. Cut capsicum into thin strips.

Boil, steam or microwave potatoes until tender; drain. Combine warm potatoes with one-third of the Herb Dressing.

Boil, steam or microwave beans until tender, rinse under cold water, drain.

Combine tomatoes with another one-third of the Herb Dressing in bowl; mix well.

Place lettuce leaves on plate, top with capsicum, potato mixture, beans, tomato mixture, flaked tuna, eggs and olives; drizzle with remaining Herb Dressing.

Herb Dressing Combine ingredients in screw-topped jar; shake well.

On the table in 40 minutes

chicken salad with
soy dressing

1 tablespoon peanut oil

4 (680g) chicken
breast fillets

1 small (400g) Chinese
cabbage, shredded

4 green onions, chopped

4 sticks celery, sliced

50g snow pea sprouts

soy dressing

1/4 cup (60ml) peanut oil

2 tablespoons soy sauce

1 teaspoon sesame oil

1 teaspoon grated
fresh ginger

1 clove garlic, crushed

1/2 teaspoon sugar

2 tablespoons lime juice

Heat oil in frying pan;
cook chicken until
browned both sides
and cooked through;
slice thinly.

Combine chicken,
cabbage, onion and
celery in bowl, top with
sprouts; drizzle with
Soy Dressing.

Soy Dressing Combine
ingredients in screw-
topped jar; shake well.

On the table in 30 minutes

mexican chicken and
chilli bean salad

2 cups (340g) chopped cooked chicken

1 cos lettuce

250g cherry tomatoes, halved

250g yellow teardrop tomatoes, halved

1 medium (200g) red capsicum, sliced

1 medium (200g) green capsicum, sliced

1 medium (170g) red onion, sliced

300g can corn kernels, rinsed, drained

2 x 300g cans red kidney beans, rinsed, drained

1 medium (250g) avocado

1/3 cup (80ml) sour cream

dressing

1/3 cup (80ml) olive oil

1 tablespoon lime juice

1 tablespoon sweet chilli sauce

1 small fresh red chilli, seeded, chopped

1 teaspoon hot paprika

On the table in 40 minutes

Combine chicken with torn lettuce leaves, tomatoes, capsicum, onion, corn, beans and Dressing in large bowl; mix gently.
Scoop flesh from the avocado; mash well with fork. Serve salad topped with mashed avocado and sour cream.
Dressing Combine ingredients in screw-topped jar; shake well.

pasta salad with

pesto dressing

500g bow-tie pasta

200g mozzarella cheese

100g sliced hot salami, cut into strips

1 cup (150g) drained sliced sun-dried tomatoes in oil

1/2 cup (80g) black olives, seeded, chopped

1/4 cup chopped fresh chives

2 tablespoons pine nuts, toasted

pesto dressing

1/3 cup (80ml) olive oil

1 tablespoon lime juice

1/2 cup loosely packed fresh basil leaves

1 tablespoon grated parmesan cheese

1 teaspoon sugar

On the table in 40 minutes

Cook pasta in large saucepan of boiling water, uncovered, until just tender; drain. Rinse under cold water; drain well. Slice cheese; cut into strips. Combine pasta with cheese, salami, tomatoes, olives and chives in large bowl. Just before serving, toss Pesto Dressing through pasta mixture; sprinkle with nuts.

Pesto Dressing Blend or process ingredients until creamy and smooth.

48 prawn and cabbage salad with minty dressing

20 (1kg) large cooked prawns

3 cups (240g) shredded cabbage

1 cup (80g) shredded red cabbage

1 stick celery, sliced

1 (130g) Lebanese cucumber, sliced

1 medium (200g) red capsicum, sliced

dressing

$^1/_4$ cup (60ml) olive oil

$^1/_4$ cup (60ml) orange juice

2 tablespoons lemon juice

$1^1/_2$ teaspoons fish sauce

$^1/_4$ cup chopped fresh mint leaves

2 teaspoons sugar

Shell and devein prawns, leaving tails intact. Combine ingredients in large bowl; pour over Dressing, mix gently. **Dressing** Combine ingredients in screw-topped jar; shake well.

On the table in 50 minutes

chicken, asparagus
and chickpea salad

*8 (880g) chicken
thigh fillets*

*250g asparagus,
trimmed*

*425g can chickpeas,
rinsed, drained*

*1 medium (170g) red
onion, sliced thinly*

1/3 cup (80ml) olive oil

*1 tablespoon
balsamic vinegar*

*1 teaspoon mild
English mustard*

*1 tablespoon chopped
fresh oregano*

On the table in 35 minutes

Griddle-fry (or grill or barbecue) chicken until browned both sides
and cooked through; cut each fillet into 3 pieces.
Boil, steam or microwave asparagus until just tender; drain. Rinse
under cold water; drain well.
Gently toss chicken and asparagus in large bowl with chickpeas,
onion and combined remaining ingredients.

50 lima bean, tomato and
rocket salad

9 large (800g) egg tomatoes

2 x 300g cans lima beans,
rinsed, drained

1 medium (170g) red onion,
sliced thinly

120g rocket, trimmed,
chopped roughly

2 tablespoons slivered
almonds, toasted

dressing

2 cloves garlic, crushed

3/4 cup (180ml) olive oil

1/2 cup (125ml) lemon juice

1/4 cup chopped fresh parsley

1 1/2 tablespoons sugar

3 teaspoons sweet paprika

1 teaspoon chilli powder

Halve tomatoes lengthways,
remove seeds, slice
tomato thinly. Combine
tomato, beans, onion,
rocket and Dressing in
large bowl; mix well.
Serve topped with nuts.
Dressing Combine
ingredients in screw-topped
jar; shake well.

On the table in 30 minutes

hot pastrami and
artichoke salad

600 sliced pastrami

1/4 cup (60ml) olive oil

2 x 400g cans
artichoke hearts,
drained, quartered

1/3 cup (75g)
caster sugar

1 1/4 cups (310ml)
dry red wine

1 medium (200g)
red capsicum,
sliced

1/2 cup (80g)
black olives,
seeded

1/4 cup shredded
fresh basil leaves

300g rigatoni

15 small fresh basil
leaves, extra

Cut pastrami into thin strips. Heat oil in saucepan; cook artichokes,
stirring, until browned lightly. Add pastrami, sugar and wine;
simmer, uncovered, 3 minutes. Add capsicum, olives and shredded
basil; cook, uncovered, 2 minutes.

Meanwhile, cook pasta in large pan of boiling water, uncovered,
until just tender; drain.

Combine pasta with pastrami mixture and extra basil leaves.

On the table in 45 minutes

tuna

and braised onion salad

¹/₄ cup (60ml) olive oil

30g butter

3 large (600g) brown onions, sliced

2 tablespoons red wine vinegar

4 (600g) tuna steaks

120g rocket, trimmed

350g spinach, trimmed, shredded

Heat oil and butter in heavy-based medium saucepan; cook onion, covered, stirring occasionally, about 20 minutes or until onion is very soft. Add vinegar; simmer, uncovered, 1 minute. Remove onion from pan.
Add tuna to same pan; cook, uncovered, until tuna is cooked as desired. Remove tuna from pan; cut into pieces. Serve warm tuna with braised onion, rocket and spinach.

On the table in 50 minutes

54 baked fetta and roasted
tomato pasta salad

300g firm fetta cheese, chopped

1/2 cup (125ml) olive oil

500g cherry tomatoes

375g penne

1/4 cup (40g) pine nuts, toasted

1/2 cup firmly packed small fresh basil leaves

1/2 cup (60g) black olives, seeded, sliced

On the table in 30 minutes

Place cheese in large piece of foil; bring sides of foil up around cheese, drizzle with 2 tablespoons of the oil. Enclose cheese in foil; place parcel at one end of shallow baking dish. Combine tomatoes with 1 tablespoon of the remaining oil in same baking dish. Bake, uncovered, in very hot oven about 15 minutes or until tomatoes are soft.

Meanwhile, cook pasta in large saucepan of boiling water, uncovered, until just tender; drain. Combine pasta with tomatoes, cheese and any pan juices in large bowl; stir through remaining oil, pine nuts, basil and olives.

crunchy
blue cheese salad

100g firm blue
vein cheese

4 thick slices
brown bread

30g butter

1 tablespoon olive oil

1 clove garlic, crushed

1 cos lettuce

1 mignonette lettuce

100g cherry
tomatoes, halved

dressing

1 teaspoon
dry mustard

2 cloves garlic,
crushed

2 teaspoons sugar

1 tablespoon milk

2 tablespoons olive oil

1 tablespoon
white vinegar

Cut cheese into 1.5cm cubes. Remove crusts
from bread, cut bread into 1cm cubes. Heat
butter and oil in large frying pan; cook garlic
and bread, stirring, until croutons are browned
all over; drain on absorbent paper.

Place lettuce leaves in dish; top with cheese,
croutons and tomato; drizzle with Dressing.

Dressing Combine ingredients in screw-topped
jar; shake well.

On the table in 30 minutes

smoked salmon, avocado and
udon salad

250g udon

300g sliced smoked salmon

90g snow pea sprouts

2 tablespoons chopped
fresh chives

1 small (100g) red onion,
chopped finely

2 small (400g) avocados,
chopped finely

1/3 cup (80ml) light olive oil

2 tablespoons rice vinegar

1 tablespoon lime juice

2 teaspoons wasabi paste

Cook noodles in large
saucepan of boiling water,
uncovered, until just tender;
drain. Rinse under cold
water; drain well.
Separate smoked salmon
slices; cut into small strips.
Just before serving, gently
toss noodles and salmon
in large bowl with snow
pea sprouts, chives, onion,
avocado and combined
remaining ingredients.

On the table in 35 minutes

58 warm mustard chicken and
potato salad

2 tablespoons olive oil

25 (1kg) tiny new potatoes, halved

4 bacon rashers, chopped

1 large cooked chicken

1/2 cup (125ml) sour cream

1/3 cup (80ml) mayonnaise

2 tablespoons seeded mustard

1/4 cup finely chopped fresh chives

Combine oil and potatoes in large baking dish; bake, uncovered, in very hot oven 25 minutes, turning once during cooking.
Meanwhile, cook bacon in large heated oiled frying pan until crisp, drain on absorbent paper.
Remove and discard skin and bones from chicken; chop chicken meat roughly.
Gently toss potatoes, bacon and chicken in large bowl with cream, mayonnaise, mustard and chives.

On the table in 45 minutes

mango chutney lamb

with rocket snap pea salad

1/3 cup (80ml) yogurt

1/3 cup (120g) mango chutney

1/3 cup (80ml) mild chilli sauce

12 (780g) lamb cutlets

250g sugar snap peas

150g rocket, trimmed

1/4 cup (60ml) olive oil

2 tablespoons balsamic vinegar

Combine yogurt, chutney and sauce in bowl.
Griddle-fry (or grill or barbecue) lamb, brushing with yogurt mixture frequently, until browned on both sides and cooked as desired.
Meanwhile, boil, steam or microwave peas until just tender. Rinse peas under cold water; drain.
Toss peas and rocket in large bowl with combined oil and vinegar. Serve rocket snap pea salad with lamb.

On the table in 45 minutes

glossary

bacon rashers also known as slices of bacon; made from pork side, cured and smoked.
streaky bacon: the fatty end of a bacon rasher (slice), without the lean (eye) meat.

beef, rib-eye steak (scotch fillet) comes from the back of the carcase over the ribs. Boneless sirloin (New York) or rump centre cut can also be used.

bok choy also called pak choi or Chinese white cabbage; has a fresh, mild mustard taste and is good braised or in stir-fries. Baby bok choy is also available.

butter use salted or unsalted ("sweet") butter; 125g is equal to 1 stick butter.

buttermilk low-fat milk cultured to give a slightly sour, tangy taste; low-fat yogurt can be substituted.

cabanossi a ready-to-eat sausage; also known as cabana.

capsicum also known as bell pepper, sweet pepper or, simply, pepper. Seeds and membranes should be discarded before use.

cheese
bocconcini: small rounds of fresh "baby" mozzarella, a delicate, semi-soft, white cheese traditionally made in Italy from buffalo milk. Spoils rapidly so must be kept under refrigeration, in brine, for not more than 1 or 2 days.

fetta: Greek in origin; a crumbly textured goat or sheep milk cheese with a sharp, salty taste.
haloumi: a firm, cream-coloured sheep milk cheese matured in brine; somewhat like a minty, salty fetta in flavour, haloumi can be grilled or fried, briefly, without breaking down.

chicken tenderloin thin strip of tender meat lying just under the breast.

chickpeas also called garbanzos, hummus or channa; an irregularly round, sandy-coloured legume used extensively in Mediterranean and Middle-Eastern cooking.

chilli sauce, sweet a comparatively mild Thai-type commercial sauce made from red chillies, sugar, garlic and vinegar.

chinese barbecued pork also known as char siew. Traditionally cooked in special ovens, this pork has a sweet-sticky coating made from soy sauce, sherry, five-spice and hoisin sauce. It is available from Asian food stores.

chinese broccoli also known as gai lum.

choy sum also known as flowering bok choy or flowering white cabbage.

couscous a fine, grain-like cereal product, made from semolina.

dill pickles pickled cucumbers.

eggplant also known as aubergine.

fish sauce also called nam pla or nuoc nam; made from pulverised salted fermented fish, most often anchovies. Has a pungent smell and strong taste; use sparingly. There are many kinds, of varying intensity.

five-spice powder a fragrant mixture of ground clove, cinnamon, star anise, Sichuan pepper and fennel seeds.

ginger, fresh also known as green or root ginger.

hoisin sauce a thick, sweet and spicy Chinese paste made from salted fermented soy beans, onions and garlic; used as a marinade or baste, or to add flavour to stir-fries and barbecued or roasted meat and vegetable dishes.

kumara Polynesian name of orange- or white-fleshed sweet potato often confused with yam.

lamb, mini roast (trim lamb round or topside) comes from the chump and leg, eye of loin and loin.

lebanese cucumber short, slender and thin-skinned; this variety is also known as the European or burpless cucumber.

lemon grass a tall, clumping, lemon-smelling and -tasting, sharp-edged grass; the white lower part of each stem is chopped and used in Asian cooking or for tea.

lemon pepper seasoning
a blend of crushed black pepper, lemon, and several herbs and spices.

mint jelly a condiment usually served with roast lamb; packaged or homemade jelly flavoured with mint flakes.

mustard
seeded: also known as wholegrain. A French-style coarse-grain mustard made from crushed mustard seeds and Dijon-style French mustard.

dijon: a hot, French mustard, creamy and full-flavoured.

oil
macadamia: a mono-unsaturated oil extracted from macadamia nuts.

olive: mono-unsaturated; made from the pressing of tree-ripened olives. Especially good for everyday cooking and as an ingredient in salad dressings. Extra Light or Light describes the mild flavour, not the fat levels.

peanut: pressed from ground peanuts; most commonly used oil in Asian cooking because of its high smoke point.

sesame: made from roasted, crushed, white sesame seeds; a flavouring rather than a cooking medium.

vegetable: any of a number of oils sourced from plants rather than animal fats.

pastrami a highly seasoned cured and smoked beef, usually cut from the round; ready to eat when purchased.

potato
tiny new: also known as cocktails or chats.

prawns also known as shrimp.

prosciutto salt-cured, air-dried (unsmoked), pressed ham; usually sold in paper-thin slices, ready to eat.

pumpkin, butternut pear-shaped with golden skin and orange flesh.

radish a root vegetable with a mild to pungent flavour.

snow peas also called mange tout ("eat all").

sugar snap peas small pods with small, formed peas inside; eaten whole.

sultanas golden raisins.

sambal oelek (also ulek or olek) Indonesian in origin; a salty paste made from ground chillies.

scallops a bivalve mollusc; we use scallops with the coral (roe) attached.

spinach correct name for spinach; the green vegetable often called spinach is correctly known as Swiss chard, silverbeet or seakale.

sugar we used coarse, granulated table sugar, also known as crystal sugar, unless otherwise specified.

brown: granulated sugar retaining molasses for its colour and flavour.

caster: also known as superfine or powdered sugar.

tomato sauce also known as ketchup or catsup; a flavoured condiment made from tomatoes, vinegar and spices.

vinegar
balsamic: authentic only from the province of Modena, Italy. Made from a regional wine of white Trebbiano grapes specially processed then aged in antique wooden casks to give its exquisite pungent flavour. The longer it is aged, the more expensive it is to buy.

brown malt: made from fermented malt and beech shavings.

red wine: based on fermented red wine.

rice wine: made from fermented rice.

tarragon: white wine vinegar infused with fresh tarragon.

wasabi an Asian horseradish used to make a fiery sauce traditionally served with Japanese raw fish dishes.

zucchini also known as courgette.

index

facts and figures

These conversions are approximate only, but the difference between an exact and the approximate conversion of various liquid and dry measures is minimal and will not affect your cooking results.

Measuring equipment

The difference between one country's measuring cups and another's is, at most, within a 2 or 3 teaspoon variance. (For the record, 1 Australian metric measuring cup holds approximately 250ml.) The most accurate way of measuring dry ingredients is to weigh them. For liquids, use a clear glass or plastic jug having metric markings.

Note: NZ, Canada, USA and UK all use 15ml tablespoons. Australian tablespoons measure 20ml.

All cup and spoon measurements are level.

How to measure

When using graduated measuring cups, shake dry ingredients loosely into the appropriate cup. Do not tap the cup on a bench or tightly pack the ingredients unless directed to do so. Level the top of measuring cups and measuring spoons with a knife. When measuring liquids, place a clear glass or plastic jug having metric markings on a flat surface to check accuracy at eye level.

Dry Measures

metric	imperial
15g	1/2 oz
30g	1oz
60g	2oz
90g	3oz
125g	4oz (1/4 lb)
155g	5oz
185g	6oz
220g	7oz
250g	8oz (1/2 lb)
280g	9oz
315g	10oz
345g	11oz
375g	12oz (3/4 lb)
410g	13oz
440g	14oz
470g	15oz
500g	16oz (1lb)
750g	24oz (1 1/2 lb)
1kg	32oz (2lb)

We use large eggs having an average weight of 60g.

Liquid Measures

metric	imperial
30ml	1 fluid oz
60ml	2 fluid oz
100ml	3 fluid oz
125ml	4 fluid oz
150ml	5 fluid oz (1/4 pint/1 gill)
190ml	6 fluid oz
250ml (1cup)	8 fluid oz
300ml	10 fluid oz (1/2 pint)
500ml	16 fluid oz
600ml	20 fluid oz (1 pint)
1000ml (1litre)	1 3/4 pints

Helpful Measures

metric	imperial
3mm	1/8 in
6mm	1/4 in
1cm	1/2 in
2cm	3/4 in
2.5cm	1in
6cm	2 1/2 in
8cm	3in
20cm	8in
23cm	9in
25cm	10in
30cm	12in (1ft)

Oven Temperatures

These oven temperatures are only a guide. Always check the manufacturer's manual.

	°C(Celsius)	°F(Fahrenheit)	Gas Mark
Very slow	120	250	1
Slow	150	300	2
Moderately slow	160	325	3
Moderate	180 –190	350 – 375	4
Moderately hot	200 – 210	400 – 425	5
Hot	220 – 230	450 – 475	6
Very hot	240 – 250	500 – 525	7

at your fingertips

These elegant slipcovers store up to 10 mini books and make the books instantly accessible.

And the metric measuring cups and spoons make following our recipes a piece of cake.

Book Holder
Australia and overseas: $8.95 (incl. GST).

Metric Measuring Set
Australia: $6.50 (incl. GST).
New Zealand: $A8.00.
Elsewhere: $A9.95.
Prices include postage and handling. This offer is available in all countries.

Photocopy and complete coupon below

Mail or fax Photocopy and complete the coupon below and post to:
ACP Books Reader Offer, ACP Publishing, GPO Box 4967, Sydney NSW 2001, *or* fax to: (02) 9267 4967.

Phone Have your credit card details ready, then phone 136 116 (Mon-Fri, 8.00am-6.00pm; Sat, 8.00am-6.00pm).

Australian residents We accept the credit cards listed on the coupon, money orders and cheques.

Overseas residents We accept the credit cards listed on the coupon, drafts in $A drawn on an Australian bank, and also British, New Zealand and U.S. cheques in the currency of the country of issue. Credit card charges are at the exchange rate current at the time of payment.

☐ **Book Holder**   ☐ **Metric Measuring Set**
Please indicate number(s) required.

Mr/Mrs/Ms _____

Address _____

_____

Postcode _____ Country _____

Ph: Business hours ( ) _____

I enclose my cheque/money order for $ _____ payable to ACP Publishing.

OR: please charge $ _____ to my   ☐ Bankcard   ☐ Mastercard

☐ Visa   ☐ American Express   ☐ Diners Club

Expiry date _____ /_____

| | | | | | | | | | | | | | | | | |

Card number

Cardholder's signature _____

Please allow up to 30 days delivery within Australia.
Allow up to 6 weeks for overseas deliveries.
Both offers expire 31/12/05. HLMS04.

Food director Pamela Clark
Assistant food editor Kathy McGarry
Assistant recipe editor Elizabeth Hooper

ACP BOOKS
Editorial director Susan Tomnay
Creative director Hieu Chi Nguyen
Concept design & Designer Jackie Richa
Publishing manager (sales) Brian Cearnes
Sales & marketing coordinator Caroline Lc
Publishing manager (rights & new projects
 Jane Hazell
Marketing manager Sarah Cave
Pre-press by Harry Palmer
Production manager Carol Currie
Business manager Seymour Cohen
Business analyst Martin Howes
Chief executive officer John Alexander
Group publisher Pat Ingram
Publisher Sue Wannan
Editor-in-chief Deborah Thomas
Produced by ACP Books, Sydney.
Printing by Dai Nippon Printing in Korea.
Published by ACP Publishing Pty Limited, 54 Park St, Sydney; GPO Box 4088, Sydne NSW 1028. Ph: (02) 9282 8618
Fax: (02) 9267 9438.
www.acpbooks.com.au
acpbooks@acp.com.au
To order books phone 136 116.
Send recipe enquiries to Recipeenquiries@acp.com.au
Australia Distributed by Network Services, GPO Box 4088, Sydney, NSW 1028.
Ph: (02) 9282 8777 Fax: (02) 9264 3278.
United Kingdom Distributed by Australian Consolidated Press (UK), Moulton Park Bus Centre, Red House Road, Moulton Park, Northampton, NN3 6AQ. Ph: (01604) 497 5 Fax: (01604) 497 533 acpukltd@aol.com
Canada Distributed by Whitecap Books Ltd 351 Lynn Ave, North Vancouver, BC, V7J 2(Ph: (604) 980 9852 Fax: (604) 980 8197
customerservice@whitecap.ca
www.whitecap.ca
New Zealand Distributed by Netlink Distribu. Company, ACP Media Centre, Cnr Fanshaw and Beaumont Streets, Westhaven, Aucklar PO Box 47906, Ponsonby, Auckland, NZ.
Ph: (9) 366 9966 ask@ndcnz.co.nz
South Africa Distributed by PSD Promotions 30 Diesel Road, Isando, Gauteng, Johannesburg; PO Box 1175, Isando, 1600, Gauteng, Johannesburg. Ph: (27 11) 392 606 Fax: (27 11) 392 6079/80 orders@psdprom.cc

Make it Tonight: Salads.
Includes index.
ISBN 1 86396 144 5

1. Salads. 2. Cookery – Australia. I. Title: Australian Women's Weekly. (Series: Austra Women's Weekly Make it Tonight mini serie

641.83

© ACP Publishing Pty Limited 1999
ABN 18 053 273 546

First published 1999. Reprinted 2002, 200

Cover: Classic chef's salad, page 22.
Stylist: Michelle Noerianto
Photographer: Rob Taylor
Back cover: on left, Grilled haloumi, tomatc and eggplant salad, page 39; on right, Chicken salad with soy dressing, page 44.